How To Chat Up Women

Stewart Ferris

SUMMERSDALE

Summersdale Publishers Ltd
46 West Street
Chichester
West Sussex
PO19 1RP
United Kingdom

Printed and bound in Great Britain.

ISBN 1 84024 044 X

Contents

Introduction

Men and women

Men are sexual bulldozers. Women, to continue the metaphor, are sexual window boxes. Try gardening a window box with a bulldozer, and you'll never get anywhere. Women don't go for speed and efficiency in sex, they want to be poked around gently with a trowel. Anyway, returning to the metaphor, if you're a sexual bulldozer you'd better find a big window box to put it in, otherwise you'll never grow any seedlings.

Learn the following Ten Inaccurate and Unfair Sexist Generalisations. They are vital to an understanding of the opposing sex, and will form the crutch of an infallibly smooth chat-up technique that will be developed later in the book.

 Ten Inaccurate and Unfair Sexist Generalisations:

1. They're all gagging for it, except the lesbians. (In fact, most seem to be lesbians.)

2. They're all mad. The word 'hysteria' comes from the Greek for 'womb', hence 'hysterical' means 'to have a womb'. Watch out.

3. Their sense of spacial awareness doesn't work as well as men's, which is why we have to park their cars for them.

4. They possess a 'washing-up' gene.

5. They live longer than men because men do all the work (except washing-up).

6. Their bra fastenings are designed by the same people who design the locks used in bank vaults.

7. Have I mentioned they all seem to be lesbians?

8. What have they got against men, anyway? Don't we respect them enough?

9. Women only think about having sex with their partner while they are doing it. This is the only time that men are not thinking about sex with their partner.

10. Women are all wonderfully different individuals and cannot be categorised or described by inane generalisations.

How To Treat A Woman

Use a good, durable varnish. No, just kidding.

Some men like to worship their women. They do anything and everything for them, shower them with gifts, think of them while they make love, and put them on a pedestal. This is bad for the relationship, counter-productive, and too good for them. The only time a woman should be put on a pedestal is when she's too short to reach the kitchen sink.

Any woman who is treated like a god will treat her man like a peasant. There needs to be a balance between what she gives you and what you give her. If she gives you a headache, give her gonorrhoea. If she gives you happiness, mental stability and bliss, let her off the housework once in a while.

Achieving this kind of perfect balance in a relationship can be as hard as Nelson's Column, but a relationship is like balancing on just two legs when you're drunk: lose that delicate balance and you fall into your own vomit. You have been warned.

 # Being single

To be young, free and single is to be a sad, lonely bastard. It's horrible, it's happened to all of us, and the only cure is to persuade a woman to go out with you. The right woman could come along at any time, but it won't be until it's furthest from your mind, and since getting a shag is always foremost on any man's mind this means a long wait for most of us.

While you're still single, spare a thought for those stuck in relationships. Couplings don't work without compromise, and

all those carefully nurtured habits which define your character and masculinity will have to be diluted. You have to be willing to make sacrifices, even with things as important as which films you watch: she might want to see a horrible romantic comedy, you might want to see a nice violent thriller.

So how do you cope with being single in the meantime? Normal practice is to develop a number of idiosyncratic, revolting and annoying personal habits that you can easily slide into whilst living alone. These will be a useful source of vitriolic acerbity, disparaging derogations and tautologous tendencies when you later enter into a relationship.

Recommended habits to develop whilst single:

1) Unlimited flatulence (farting).
2) Sleeping alone in a double bed so that you take up its entire area and all of the double duvet.
3) Always keeping the toilet seat up.
4) Washing-up once a month, whether you need to or not.
5) Bathing once a month, whether you need to or not.
6) Seeing how high you can fill the bin before you empty it.
7) Practising resonant choral belching for half an hour a day.
8) Thinking that flushing the toilet is the same as cleaning it.
9) Downloading *art* images from the Internet every night.
10) Buying new crockery rather than washing up, only to find there's no room in the bin.

Being single

Understanding women

If women spoke French or Spanish, that would be fine. We could learn from a phrasebook what they are saying, and respond accordingly.

For example, she may say,

'Mon aeroglisseur est plein d'anguilles'
(*My hovercraft is full of eels*),

and you could reply,

'Je n'en ai rien a foutre'
(*I don't care* — or words to that effect).
All would be comprehensible after a few lessons. But women sound as if they are speaking plain English when in fact they speak a secret code which even MI5 cannot crack.

When a woman approaches you out of the blue and asks you the time of day, she is not actually asking if you would like to sleep with her. Believe it or not she really does want to know what time it is. When a shop girl offers you assistance, she is not making a pass at you, even if it obviously seems that way. What she wants to know is whether she can help you in her professional capacity.

Here are some common women's phrases and their true meanings:

1. She says:
Would you like fries with that, sir?

You think she means:
Would you like to come and meet me in half an hour behind the dustbin compound for a snog?

She actually means:
Would you like fries with that, sir?

2. She says:
Can I just have one pint of milk today?

You think she means:
My husband's away, so I'll be needing less of your milk and more of your renowned sexual services.

She actually means:
Can I just have one pint of milk today?

3. She says:
Would you like to massage my naked body?

You think she means:
Would you like fries with that?

She actually means:
Can I just have one pint of milk today?

What is required from men, therefore, is the ability to think and to communicate on two levels. Firstly, on the male, one-track sexual level which we are all used to and which enables us to cope with most situations; and secondly on a female level, where nothing is as it seems.

Conflict

Men often make the mistake of expecting women to behave in the same way as men. Rationality and logic are standard fittings that come with facial hair and testes. With breasts, they are optional extras. But hang on, this is a little unfair. Women have their own rationales and their own logic. Their set their priorities differently to men, and that is why it's so easy for misunderstandings to occur. Put simply and objectively, only important things are important to men; unimportant things are important to women. Remember this when disagreement flares, and you'll be able to dampen the

flames in no time with a broad minded, fair and patronising attempt at appeasement.

To avoid conflict, always listen to her . . . she may test you later. There's nothing worse than nodding politely during her monologue in the pub, occasionally looking her in the eye and smiling, while all the time concentrating on the football match on the pub's telly, only to be asked questions about her problems afterwards. 'So what should I do about it?' she will plead, just as the referee tries to break up an interesting fight.

You have two choices:

1. Own up. Tell her you weren't listening, apologise profusely, and join a dating agency the next morning.

2. Guess at what she was talking about. Her hair is a pretty likely topic, so if you say, 'I think you should dye it blonde,' at least you'll be in with a chance of salvation. If it turns out she was telling you about her pregnant pet dog, apologise profusely and join a dating agency the next morning.

Ideally, give her regular feedback throughout her monologues. This will make her feel appreciated, and creates the impression that you are not bored. Nods, grins, mmms, and sneezes will all show to her that you're still alive behind that glazed expression. She'll think that you're excited, riveted and enthusiastic about what she is saying. Women love good listeners.

When her monologue comes to an end, don't say, 'Hurry up, the landlord's about to throw us out.' Just kiss her softly in front of the fire . . . no, actually, that comes later. Find out how much she's going to charge you, first.

♀ The basics of chatting-up ♀

Most people find it hard to approach a member of the opposite sex. In fact, those who say they find it easy are probably either famous pop stars or liars. People are surprised when they hear that an incredibly attractive person finds it hard to 'chat someone up'. If they find it hard, it is to say they lack confidence. Therefore good looks do not necessarily endow confidence in a man. It really has nothing to do with physical characteristics: to approach someone you need courage, and this can be bought in handy bottles and cans at pubs and off licences.

Another common hangup is the difficulty in talking coherently to the opposite sex. You might find it easy talking to your friends but as soon as you have to talk to a woman the words cease to flow and you're left feeling self conscious and embarrassed. You lose control of your mouth and all the wrong words come out.

Instead of 'I'd like to shag you', you can only stammer the words 'Hi, how are you?' Your nerves have blown it for you. She tells you her name, and again you want to ask her for a shag, but all you can tell her is your own name. And so the conversation progresses. You really want to cut the crap and tell her what you're after, because if she's not after that you're wasting your time. She starts to like you, and thinks you're an interesting person, but bedded bliss doesn't seem to be moving towards you very quickly.

You try one more time to ask her back to your place for a shag, but the words come out as, 'I'm not the sort of person who does it on a first date,' because that's what you're brain thinks is in your longer term interests. 'That's a shame,' she replies, 'because I was going to offer you a shag. Looks like I've been wasting my time.' And off she goes. Happens all the time.

It's very important to control your brain and say what you want to say in order to avoid portraying an erroneous persona. But controlling your brain is just one of a myriad of things that have to be carried out simultaneously when chatting-up. Obviously the loins have to be dampened until they are needed, your body language will be under observation, and even the pace of your breathing can make or break the situation. These aspects will all have to mastered individually, and then combined to produce the polished performer that you want to be.

An excessive intake of alcohol will easily keep little Johnny Sausage from trying to make an early appearance while you're flirting with her in the bar, but it will rule out one or two interesting options later on.

Ten ways of dousing the fire in your loins until her furnace is ready to be stoked:

1. Tie a heavy weight around it.
2. Try looking at her only from the neck upwards (takes a bit of practice).
3. Keep the conversation topics *clean*.
4. Try looking at the barmaids only from the neck upwards.
5. Don't look at the way she handles her long, narrow glass.
6. Try to remember some recent sports results.
7. Think about moustaches.
8. Tell her it's actually a gun in your pocket.
9. Encourage her to be unpleasant to you.
10. Put a hat on your lap.

Psychology

This, in a sense, is what chatting-up is all about. There is a very fine line between a woman thinking you're a bit of a jerk but probably alright underneath, and her thinking you're a total git. What you say, how you say it, and your appearance are vital factors in swaying her opinion either way. If she finds you interesting, you'll probably need to change your sheets tomorrow. If you're boring, the sheets will have to wait a few more weeks.

You are particularly at risk of boring her if you think you have led a fascinating life. Try starting off the evening with a lengthy monologue all about yourself, about the famous people you went to school with, how fast your car is, and the story of your previous disastrous relationships, and see how far you get. Reciting your unpublishable autobiography to a stranger in a nightclub will bore her to tears.

Paradoxically, she'll come away thinking you're interesting if you have asked questions about her, and have consistently shown interest in her life. When chatting-up, never use the first person, always talk about her. If she asks about you, answer fully enough not to sound evasive, but don't use her question as a springboard to repeat everything you told your psychiatrist the night before when you asked him why you never score. Answer her question and then relate the topic back to her. She will probably have asked the question out of politeness rather than out of genuine interest, and will welcome the opportunity to start talking once more about herself.

Another cardinal rule is never to go on about an ex-girlfriend. Mentioning how attractive she was, how you never really

meant to be unfaithful to her, and how every time you were unfaithful it actually served to strengthen your love for her, will only antagonise your date. If you must mention an ex-girlfriend, it will suffice to say how long the relationship lasted and when it finished. Avoid referring to the ex-girlfriend in a totally negative way: your date may then start wondering whether you would refer to her in the same way once she eventually dumps you.

An important rule of dating is never to let a woman know how desperate you are. Drooling all over a woman will probably make her sick. It is all a matter of balance: keep the scales level and you stand a better chance. If a woman comes on strong, don't instantly fall at her feet, show a certain degree of self control. Then fall at her feet.

Image

Your image is the way people perceive you. If no one ever even notices you, then you probably haven't got an image at all. Don't worry — it's good to start with a clean slate.

For the rest of you, take a long, hard look in the mirror and ask yourself what image are you portraying? Are you, for example, the sort of sad, lonely, worrier who stares in the mirror at length wondering how they can improve their image? Or does your mirror swoon at the sight of you, forcing you to resuscitate it with a passionate embrace? Or can you see yourself objectively, spot aspects of your image that are attractive and those which might deter women from using you as a fun, convenient leisure facility?

The main component parts of your image:

1. Trousers. Whether or not you wear any at all says a lot about you. Jeans are popular, but their style, condition and fit can say completely opposite things about you. Streaky white stonewashed denim tells the world that you probably lost your sense of taste in a freak knitting accident. Levis 501s with a leather belt, on the other hand, will not deter women from your trouser area.

2. Hairstyle. Again, do you have any? If so, what message is it giving out? Hair is a surprisingly eloquent communicator, with the capability of saying anything from 'You'd better cross to the other side of the street before I start talking to you about my train set', to 'Single man, 23, loves sex, and is looking for any woman for romance. Must have good teeth.'

3. Shoes. What do they say about you? If your white socks are visible beneath your sandals, you could be in urgent need of a fashion transplant. Only wear shoes that are appropriate for what you're doing: training shoes are only for sport, walking boots are only for stuffing in the back of your car in case you run out of petrol and have to walk to a garage, and kicker boots are for kicking.

4. Hats. Best to stick to just one hat at a time, if any, and make sure you've managed to put it on properly. Too many hat wearers these days do not own mirrors. This is a false economy: they put on a hat, have no idea how it looks, and spend all day wearing a baseball cap backwards, looking like one of the less intellectual characters from *Dumb and Dumber*.

5. Mood. What sort of mood are you in? Are you happy with your wash? Look closer . . . etc. Being moody is generally cooler than being happy, but it's not much fun.

6. Fingernails. Dirty or clean, short or long? And don't forget to think about your fingernails, too.

7. Dance style. Do you go to those modern torture chambers disguised on the exterior as nightclubs and rave enthusiastically to the sound of machine gun fire and strangled cats, or do you waltz elegantly (albeit alone) to your Sing-along-a-Strauss CD? People are attracted to different dance styles — usually it will be the styles you have never mastered.

8. Jewellery. Gold watch, bracelets, rings, and tinted gold glasses say much more about your taste than words can ever do, which is useful if you have a speech impediment.

9. Pepsi or Coke? Do you think it matters which one you're seen drinking? I don't think so.

10. Glasses. Big plastic ones, small wire-rimmed ones, or beer glasses? Which sort you choose may help determine whether you can see properly.

There are even more basic questions: do I have bad breath or unsightly personal habits? Filtering your breath through a gas mask is often impractical, but regular brushing of your masticators will help. If your personal habits are unsightly, the solution is simple: keep them out of sight.

A few instant turn-offs:

1. Unpleasant body odour
2. Greasy hair
3. 'Dull' hair
4. Dirty clothes
5. Unfashionable clothes
6. Picking one's nose
7. Picking someone else's nose
8. Scratching one's extremities

When inventing a new image for yourself, try not to stray too far from your inherent personality. If you're naturally a quiet chap, and you want to develop a 'loud' image, don't try to become a town crier all at once. Change your image gently by turning up your radio a little bit more than usual, and by complaining in restaurants at a sufficient volume for the waiter actually to hear you.

Everyone feels stupid with a new image for the first few days . . . but you're probably right to feel that way. Oh well.

Is it unfair that chatting-up is dependent upon the right image for success? Of course it is, but that's life. It's just a big act from start to finish — 'All the world's a stage, and I've got the biggest part' as Shakespeare didn't quite say. Hide behind the right image and women will accept you. Get behind the wrong one and the only thing to welcome you with open arms is obscurity.

Attracting someone involves selling yourself, but standing in the pub with a 'for sale' sign on your back has a poor track record of success. Selling yourself really means making yourself attractive to the prospective client. In a chat-up situation, the first thirty seconds of contact are all you have to grab her attention and win her over. It's similar to a TV advert: you are the product and the woman is the market.

What might your best selling points be?

- No previous owners.

- Your rifle has only been fired in practice, never at the enemy.

- Fully housetrained.

- Inexperienced, but eager to learn.

Would a woman become hooked by this sales pitch, or would you have to use a fishing rod? Try to make a list of your own points and refine them into a slick, glossy advert. Wherever possible, try to use these selling points. But if all else fails, get your rod out.

You must value yourself. If you find this difficult, go to an auctioneer for an expert opinion. Your value can be measured either in moral terms or in feet and inches. Increasing your sense of self worth is not difficult: if you have ever excelled in anything, try to bring that to mind before you begin chatting-up. This is not in order to tell her all about it, but to boost your self-confidence generally.

Things at which you may have excelled:

1. The highest pisser on the school wall.
2. Managing to keep the same underwear on for the longest without washing it.
3. Eating the biggest bogey.
4. Being able to belch and fart at the same time.
5. Not being able to get a woman.
6. Wondering why you can't get a woman.
7. Wondering if it has anything to do with the first four achievements (above).
8. Wasting days at a time wallowing in depression and regret that the first four achievements have blown all your chances.
10. Avoiding the number 9 wherever possible.

If you have successfully chatted someone up before but are nervous about doing it with someone else, boost your confidence by remembering how you did it the first time . . . and how the same disasters are unlikely to occur twice in a row.

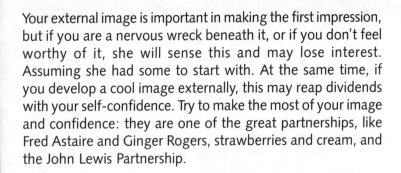

Your external image is important in making the first impression, but if you are a nervous wreck beneath it, or if you don't feel worthy of it, she will sense this and may lose interest. Assuming she had some to start with. At the same time, if you develop a cool image externally, this may reap dividends with your self-confidence. Try to make the most of your image and confidence: they are one of the great partnerships, like Fred Astaire and Ginger Rogers, strawberries and cream, and the John Lewis Partnership.

Fashion

Fashions come and go year by year, month by month and even week by week. Whatever is in vogue on breakfast television this morning is unlikely to be in fashion after lunch. This not only applies to clothes, but to music, cars, food and even lager.

So what has this got to do with chatting-up women? Well, if you wear a duffel coat and trousers that don't reach your ankles and wonder why people who follow the latest silly fashions get off with more girls than you, it might be wise to think about the shallowness and fickleness of some girls. They may, in your opinion, be foolish to fall for men whose only interests are pop music and clothes, whereas you may be knowledgeable about modern railway systems and insects, but if you want them to take any notice of you it will be necessary to change your style. Swallow your pride, your principles, and a few pints, try to look like everyone else, and acceptance by the female fraternity should soon follow.

Lack of fashion sense can usually be compensated for by an appealing charisma and charming eccentricity, but this normally comes with age, along with incontinence and strange eyebrows, so it's not really worth waiting for.

Hair

There is no point in printing a guide that tells you exactly how to have your hair cut. The only thing to do is to look closely at other people and try to get a haircut similar to theirs. Once you do this, make sure you check the current fashions regularly. Otherwise you may end up like the thousands of middle-aged men who today still wear their teddy-boy's haircut from the Fifties, or the famous ageing hippies whose fashion clocks stopped in 1972. Every six to twelve months is a good time to review your hairstyle if you have made it particularly fashionable. Otherwise, play safe with a short, neat 'business-like' haircut that requires little attention and is less likely to go out of fashion quickly . . . because it was never *in* fashion in the first place.

There is a bewildering range of hair care products available suitable for all hair types: shampoos, conditioners, gels etc.

Although they may say they are for men, they are actually intended for women, only the *wo* has fallen off the *man*. Every real man knows that getting rained on once in a while is more than adequate to drown any unwanted squatters on your scalp.

The most vital thing to recognise if you are having trouble chatting-up women is whether you have 'square' hair. If it is combed with an immaculate side parting that shows a clear line of scalp from your ear to the back of your head, or if it is brushed straight down to your eyebrows in the same sensible way you have done it since you were a child, it might be time for a change. You may not want to make your hair 'trendy', but girls will otherwise perceive you as being square, which is the same as boring. They won't give you a chance. Get yourself a more outrageous haircut and give yourself a chance . . . to look really stupid.

Alcohol

The chances are that you're drunk right now while you're reading this book. Don't fall over. On the other hand, you and some mates might have decided to stay in and get sober, in which case you'll have to break ranks and get back to the pub.

Drinking gives you that little bit of Dutch courage that you need in order to approach a woman knowing that she will soon reject you in a vicious and cruel way. Booze softens the pain of rejection by enabling you to forget why you approached her in the first place, what her name was, and where you live. It is most effective in a rowdy party situation where you drink by the bottle rather than by the glass, and you can sneak outside or upstairs with a young lady. Avoid getting plastered in a public library, however, as it's difficult to keep silent.

There is less of a need for subtlety when the sharp corners of your amateurish chat-up lines are blurred by an alcoholic haze. Jokes are funnier, embarrassment is diminished, and the corniest and most blatant chat-up lines suddenly transform into aphorisms more worthy of Oscar Wilde than of Bugs Bunny.

Getting drunk is a great idea, provided it makes you randy and cute rather than violent and sick. Ask a friend which category you come under if you can't remember. Don't drink so much that you decide to drink a pint of your own urine, as this won't impress anyone. Well, it will impress *the lads* of course, but they don't count.

One of the biggest psychological blocks in chatting-up is the initial approach. A moderate amount of alcohol in your blood can make that first approach very much easier. You will be

less afraid of the consequences of rejection, and will come across as more confident and less farty (provided you can still form a coherent sentence). However, this approach can backfire if you appear to be drunk and insincere. OK, so you *are* drunk and insincere, but *she* doesn't need to know, does she?

Telephoning

Apart from the personal approach, the next most popular method of asking someone out is by using the telephone. Picking up the phone can be daunting; using it to phone a girl can be even worse. It's just as hard as asking someone out face to face, but at least you don't have to worry whether your zits are oozing puss as you speak.

Let us suppose you have met a girl and exchanged numbers. You will have given her your phone number, she will have given you her VAT number hoping it will throw you off the scent. Don't give up, track her down via the VAT office. But when should you phone after exchanging numbers? Should you play it cool and wait for her to call you? This is a dangerous psychological game, and usually lasts for about ten years. When she does finally call it will only be because she wanted to order a pizza and mis-dialled.

If you phone immediately, she'll be put off. It suggests to her that you've never had a social life before, and that maybe you could start it with her. Make her think you've already got friends to see and things to do by sitting at home for two or three days fretting, counting the hours, and desperately trying not to phone her until sufficient time has elapsed for your follow up to appear cool and laid-back.

Be prepared for the possibility that she won't remember you. She will probably have had fifteen men phoning her since the day you 'accidentally' knocked her over in the supermarket with your trolley and gallantly offered to take her to dinner as compensation. Have a copy of your CV in front of you so that you can remind her succinctly who and what you are. Don't give her too much detail however — she won't care that you represented your country in the Olympic Masturbation Relay Team.

If her response is clearly negative when you phone, don't keep pestering her on the phone each day until she agrees to meet you. Although in the old films the lover who keeps on trying despite constant rejection, declaring his love for her with flowers, gifts and phone calls, finally gets to marry her, in reality you will end up with a court injunction banning you from any contact with her. Learn when to give up. You'll get used to it.

If she sounds remotely pleased to hear from you, assuming she remembers who you are, keep the tone as casual and unimportant as you can. Don't make it sound as if your entire future happiness depends on her response, even though we all know that it does. Make it clear that you think meeting her again would be a great idea, but that it doesn't matter if she can't make it since you've got one or two other things to do. It's just that you can't remember what they are at the moment.

The conversation may be a little stilted if you or she is shy, so don't stretch the phonecall beyond a time that you can comfortably manage. A minute's dialogue can seem like a marathon if you haven't prepared a script and have difficulty in thinking and talking at the same time, so write down a list of questions and topics for discussion before you dial. It will take some practice before you choose the best structure for your 'informal chat', so don't worry if your first conversation goes something like this:

Her: Hello?

You: Hi.

Her: Hello?

You: The meat industry has suffered from the success of European political union. Discuss.

Her: Who is this?

You: It's me. Frank. I knocked you over in the supermarket at the weekend.

Her: Oh God, not you.
You: Yeh. What's your favourite flower?
Her: Self raising.

With practice you'll get it right. When people first get to know each other, there may be little in common to talk about. If a long, embarrassed pause occurs, wind up to the conversation quickly, going straight for the question,

"I'd like to take you for dinner at a restaurant this week."

or whatever the purpose of the call is. Make sure there is a purpose, by the way. Note that saying later this week is less specific than naming a particular day, and reduces her opportunity for saying no. It is always useful to avoid backing yourself into a corner by being too specific about a place (she may not like it) or a time (she may be busy) when first asking someone out. She will then reply,

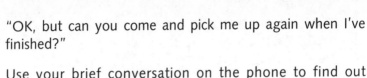

"OK, but can you come and pick me up again when I've finished?"

Use your brief conversation on the phone to find out information that may be relevant on a subsequent date. If she's a vegetarian you won't be wanting to take her to a Buffalo Grill and then on to a bullfight. If she's a classical music buff she probably won't want to be taken to hear your favourite busker who plays Beethoven on his teeth with a small spoon.

One of life's worst nightmares is plucking up the courage to ring her, only for the phone to be answered by a male voice. Try not to let your shock and disappointment show. Act cool, ask her who it was that answered the phone. If you want to sound really disinterested, tell her that her boyfriend sounds like a nice bloke. If she thanks you and agrees, you've got problems. If she says that you spoke to Hilda who has a rather deep voice, all will be well.

Excuses for phoning:

1) You're really bored because you've got no friends, and you think having sex with her would help to pass the time.

2) To ask her to a party. Clearly you haven't actually been invited to any parties, but you can always pretend it was cancelled at the last minute and take her to the scrap yard instead.

3) You met someone today who knows her and it's a small world but you wouldn't like to paint it.

4) You were wondering what size bra she wore.

5) She left some knickers behind when you last met (this obviously isn't true, but she might be spurred into jealousy by thinking she has a rival for your affections . . . and pigs might fly).

Where to go on a date

Where you choose to take your date will depend on whether you are better at communicating with words or with your body. You're obviously having trouble on the talking front if you ask her what her favourite film is, and she replied 'Kodak'. If this is the case, take her to see a film anyway and try to seduce her with bodily contact in the back row. No words need be spoken, no corny chat-up lines, just pure physical affection.

On the other hand, if she reacts to gentle contact like a cow recoiling from an electric stun gun, you're in for a verbose evening if you're going to talk her round to your way of thinking. If you take her to a bar, make sure it's a quiet one where you can hear each other talking rather than a nightclub in which you will need to lip read.

If she selects a suitable pub, make sure it's not one that is frequented by all of her ex-boyfriends, who are all fresh out of the army and desperate for a fight.

The ten worst venues for a first date:

1. Your bedroom.
2. The local car showroom.
3. Raymond's Revue Bar.
4. Your favourite underpants shop.
5. Dinner with her parents.
6. Your local pub where all your mates are waiting for you holding score cards.
7. Her wedding party.
8. The beach where her boyfriend works as a lifeguard while on probation.
9. A motorway hard shoulder.
10. Your underpants (while you're still wearing them).

The ten best venues for a first date:

1. Her bedroom.
2. Her private 'nude only' swimming pool.
3. Her favourite lingerie shop.
4. Her bed.
5. Her silk undersheets.
6. Her silk underwear (while she's wearing it).
7. A Buckingham Palace tea party.
8. Underneath a silk parachute.
9. A Caribbean cruise.
10. Her.

Handling the date

What could be more frightening than a date with a relative stranger, except perhaps a date with a strange relative? Dating a woman for the first time requires more balls than a bingo machine, so make sure you're fully loaded in that department before you go out.

Pre-date nerves can reduce a man to a quivering lump of jelly, which is fine for feeding hungry children at a birthday party, but will fail to satisfy the needs of a hungry woman. So before the date, calm yourself with controlled breathing, and try to maintain that *cool* image you have been trying for weeks to perfect. Believe it or not, she is probably just as nervous as you are. The chances are that an hour before you meet, while you're splashing after-shave into your pants, she'll be spewing up her lunch into a bucket in a final bulimic attempt to purge

herself of fat that doesn't actually exist and which, if it did exist, would make her more attractive.

During those inevitable reflective moments before the date (when you're looking in the mirror), be realistic about what you expect to happen. Pessimism from the start will rule out any nasty surprises. The worst that will happen is that she'll hate you, and turn out to be a journalist writing a feature on the worst dates she's ever had, and you come top, and no one ever wants to date you again. If you go along expecting this worst case scenario, you won't be disappointed.

Set a modest target for a first date. Rather than exchanging fluids with her, your target should be simply to exchange a few words with her before she makes a limp excuse for cutting short the date and going on her own to another bar to see if there are any *real* men with whom she can try her luck.

The next stage to aim for, if you pass the first hurdle, is to become a trusted friend of hers. If all goes well, aim for a *goodnight kiss* resulting in a *goodnight slap* after the second date, moving up to a *goodnight 'Oh go on, just a little one'* after the third date and finally a *goodnight 'Oh come on, you won't feel a thing, honest — I'll do all the work. What about if I pay you?'* after the fourth (and usually final) date.

If you kiss the side of her face on a first greeting, avoid nibbling her ears (unless you're really hungry) and keep your tongue in place . . . her make-up will be thick and fresh and won't taste too good. Be careful if you shake hands with her, as it can seem over-familiar, and try not to dribble.

If you go to get the drinks, you both have a few moments alone to compose yourselves, to let your first impressions of each other sink in, and for her to run away. If she's still there when you come back, the ice is usually broken by the following kind of dialogue:

You: Er.
Her: Sorry?
You: Eh?
Her: I said sorry.
You: What about?
Her: Nothing.
You: Oh.
Her: Hmm.
You: Nice socks.
Her: Thanks.
You: Do you wear them often?
Her: Eh?
You: Your socks.
Her: Yes, thanks.
You: Nice phone. Is it off at the moment?
Her: Yeh.
You: Do you always have it off on a first date?

When it comes to the end of the date, remember your original objective. Do you want her to respect you and give you a chance to form a long term relationship? Of course not! Go for it! Relationships that start quickly end quickly, so try to go out with a bang (or at least a little pop).

Before going for a one night stand, ask yourself if you're ready for that level of commitment. You may be with her for anything up to twelve hours, and a lot of previously hidden character traits can come out in that time. If you feel ready for such an adventure, the way you say goodbye at the 'end' of the date should indicate that this is just the beginning of something beautiful, something that will last all night. Don't let her get the wrong idea — that you don't want to sleep with her. Make sure she's aware that she has the option, and it expires very quickly if she doesn't take it up soon.

If she invites you into her house, try not to scream 'YES!' and dance a little jig up the front steps. She may just have a leaking tap that she wants you to take a look at. Once you've had a poke around inside her plumbing it will probably be time to leave. There's always a next time.

First impressions

Not to be confused with *doing impressions* of a girl, which is strictly for the professionals. *Impressing* someone is to print onto their mind a favourable image of you, one that will last long enough to override the memory of any disappointing facets she subsequently discovers about you. The first impression has to be a good one, so it will involve acting, faking and generally conning her into thinking you're someone other than your real self. It's dishonest, of course, but she'll be doing the same thing. Probably.

To take a silly example, imagine you meet a girl having just won an Olympic gold medal for setting a new farting record — her first impression of you will be of a champion, a success, and a potentially good shag. Now imagine instead that you meet her having just forced out an equally impressive jam

tart in a public toilet, walking out the door with a huge smile on your face — she'll walk the other way very quickly.

It is possible, in theory, to impress a girl with your body, but it's usually not worth the risk. Keeping your clothes on until the last possible minute is probably the safest option for most men.

Performers are always popular with women. No matter what you do, being *up there* and doing something is sexy. Even the ugliest rock stars have groupies waiting to have their underwear autographed. A good performance of some sort always makes a good first impression.

You could get noticed by the opposite gender by any of the following means:

1. Talent contest — do an exotic belly dance with your beer gut.
2. Politics — stand on a soapbox in the High Street and rant about noise pollution until someone tells you to shut up.
3. Amateur dramatics — get your *part* noticed in a production of *Hair*.
4. Village idiot — become the local nutter who stands by the road all day miming a man pushing against strong winds.
5. Rock band — learn to hold a bass guitar and become a star in a string of pubs.

Talking

Talking, regrettably, is a major component of the chatting-up process. It's where most men come unstuck. They've perfected their look, their smell, the way they walk (knuckles dragging on the ground) and they've armed themselves with a stock of infallible chat-up lines. But once they come face to face with the target, something strange happens inside the brain. It's as if the words they want to say get put through a blender somewhere between the brain and the mouth. So instead of coolly uttering,

'Shall we go and see a film?'
(To which she might reply, 'I've seen it.')

they in fact come out with,

'Shall we go and film the sea?'

Even if the first line goes smoothly, the follow up can easily become mashed, so instead of,

'So what's your favourite record?'
(To which she would reply,
'Sebastion Coe's 1500 metres.')

all that comes out is,

'Wibble wibble dribble.'

The words you say to her are clues to your personality, so getting those words right can be helpful. But worrying about getting the words right can make you tongue-tied and incoherent, making you sound like a railway porter. Then again, worrying about worrying about getting the words right can be even worse, so maybe it's just best to forget about it.

The main thing to remember on a date is don't talk about yourself. She's not interested. No one is. She's only interested in talking about herself, so let her do it. She'll love you for it. Prompt her to talk about her hair, her clothes, her job, her home town, her car (not in too much detail though - something along the lines of 'I see you drive a red car. That's a nice colour.' will be enough not to alienate her). Ask what she likes to drink, what countries she has visited, what her husband does for a living. Resist the temptation, whenever she replies to one of your questions, to turn the conversation to yourself:

You: What do you do to your hair, pretty one?
Her: I bleach it.
You: That's great. I bleach my rabbits: albinos are worth more. I'll cook you a stew one day, if you want. Tastes a bit like it's been marinated in a swimming pool, but it's alright really. Kills all the germs. Kills the rabbits too!

The 10 worst conversation topics you could choose:

1. Football.
2. Computers
3. Cars.
4. Lager.
5. Strip lighting.
6. Stripping.
7. Fighting.
8. Trains.
9. Your wife.
10. Your diseases.

If she tells you about her problems, under no circumstances try to solve them. Attempting to find a logical solution to her conundrums will result in you being swept away by her tears of frustration. Odd though it may seem, she will appreciate

sympathy more than practicality. Just give her your full attention and listen carefully, giving occasional responsive noises such as 'uhmm' or 'yes'. If you can't manage those noises, the occasional fart will let her know you're still around.

Bullshit

Since chatting-up is all about making an initial impression and creating an image of yourself, it can be a severe disadvantage if you are a nobody who has led a particularly dull life, even by the standards of the other members of the local 'Dull Society'. If you are after a quick fling, it can be worth embellishing your curriculum vitae with whatever you think will make a girl regard you as a *better pull*. For one night stands, when you're away from home or on holiday and don't expect or want to see the girl again, you can adopt an exciting but entirely false persona for the evening - librarian, stamp auctioneer, or gas meter polisher. Enjoy yourself.

Keep the bullshit realistic. Don't say you're a paediatrician and then offer to sort out her feet. Basically, don't get out of your depth, unless you are such a boring person that it's your only chance. If you have to tell a lie to impress, try to make sure you can't be caught out. If caught out, laugh it off as a rather sad, practical joke.

When on home ground or when you want the relationship to develop, play safe and keep the lies small and white. Give your job a more exciting description:

'I work in the communications business,'

or

'I'm involved in the written media,'

instead of,

'I'm a postman.'

Bullshit also applies to your attitude towards her. She may be an opera buff, she may have a fetish for Norwegian fjords and spend most of the evening reminiscing about them. Unless you are cool enough to walk away from such a bore, in which case you probably have enough confidence and experience not to need this book, you should put up with her monologue. Indeed, you should actively encourage her, asking intelligent questions about her specialist subject and pretending you have a genuine interest and maybe a little knowledge of it. Yes, you went to several operas last year (too many to name), and yes you love fjords too — your favourite is the fjord Mondeo. She will love you for it.

Sense of humour

Most women say that the most attractive thing about a man is his sense of humour, though they might have been joking. If you can make a woman laugh (at your repartee, not at you), it is likely that she will enjoy being with you. This does not mean you need to begin your evening together with a five minute stand up comedy routine combining sharp political satire with quickfire one-liners, but be lighthearted and make witty comments where appropriate.

If she has something serious to say to you, be careful not to say something you think is witty and will cheer her up but which she may interpret as insensitive flippancy. For instance,

Her: I'm really upset. My cat died today.
You: Oh dear, that's a shame . . . all those fleas are going to be homeless! Still, at least you'll probably get a refund on the catfood.

This is fine if you're trying to end a relationship, but if you think humour like that will win her love you might as well confess to being the one who ran over her cat in the first place.

Often the best way to share humour with a girl you don't know very well is to find someone nearby to laugh at, though even this method is prone to backfiring if you stray into political incorrectness by picking an *oppressed minority* type as your target, such as a Liberal politician or an estate agent. She's bound to find it funny if you see someone trying to chat-up a girl with a copy of this book behind his back, although she won't see it in the same way if she discovers *your* copy sticking out of your pocket.

Body language

We all know a little body language. At its most basic level we know the implicit differences between a smile and a frown, a 'thumbs-up' and a 'thumbs-down' or a slap in the face and a punch in the stomach. These clues enable us to understand a person's emotions or feelings. They make us feel welcome or rejected, happy or sad, without the need for any words to be spoken.

Wide, lasting smiles are usually more genuine than thin, short ones. A totally limp hand when shaking hands for the first time implies disinterest, while a firm, lingering handshake means she wants to have your babies. Listen carefully to the tone of her voice: is there a hint of enthusiasm in it, or is she talking in her sleep?

Watch out for hidden yawns, heads rolling to one side, and a blatant unwillingness to enter your *personal space*. She may defend her own personal space by placing her bag between you, facing slightly away, or by erecting a few miles of razor wire fence. Conversely, if she sits close to you and runs her hands up and down your inner thigh as she talks, it could be time to visit the family planning clinic.

Learn to interpret eye-contact. If she blinks repeatedly as she looks at you it's likely that she either has something in her eye or that she thinks you are something in her eye that won't go away. But if she holds you in her gaze, move your head closer to her and look into her eyes. The first one to laugh loses.

Physical contact

Your first move on someone has to be a subtle one, to make it easy to cover up in case it backfires, yet it has to enable her to reciprocate her feelings in a similar manner if she's gagging for it. This is where a great deal of skill is needed in reading those all important body signals.

Unfortunately many people interpret these signals differently. If you brush your hand against hers while you both stand at the bar waiting for hours to be served because there are loads of people in tonight and the pub is either short staffed or just badly managed, she might misinterpret your actions as an attempt to pickpocket her and will knee you in the balls in a most embarrassing way.

Or perhaps her handbag rubs against your bottom by accident, but you interpret this as a *come on* and start sticking your dribbling tongue in her ear, short-circuiting her tiny hearing aid and frying her brain, much to her annoyance. Be sure you have interpreted the signs correctly before *going for it*.

Timing is important. It's no use responding to her physical contact days later when she's already dating someone else. Similarly, don't pre-empt a possible move on her part with a risky one on your part (or even *with* your part). Respond quickly and smoothly if she makes physical contact by reciprocating to the same degree. Thus, if she holds your hand, hold hers. If she kisses you, kiss her. If she slaps you, duck.

It's not uncommon to leave a date thinking, *why on earth did nothing happen?* It was either because making that move seemed impossible or because she didn't fancy you. Usually the latter.

The trouble is that once the date is over, it's too late, so you have to be brave with making that first physical contact as soon as you get a chance. Making this move is tantamount to putting yourself up for sale and asking her if she will buy you. If she doesn't, you may be asking too much. Let her haggle, and see what she offers. Maybe she'll offer you a part-exchange on her ex-boyfriend? Maybe she was looking for something with a better fixtures and fittings, or perhaps a garden with a conservatory?

Rejection under these circumstances is nothing to be ashamed of. Well, it's no more shameful than any of the other forms of rejection men have to go through in their daily contacts with their opposites.

What body signs should you give out yourself? You can kiss her without warning and accept the consequences, or you can test the waters by some gentle physical contact, for instance by touching something *near* her.

Hold her hand if you are walking together (take her hand to help her over rough ground or steps, then don't let go — unless she trips and would otherwise bring you down with her), or rub her arm with your hand or with a roll of money.

Teamwork

It was Adam Smith who proved that division of the available labour force into specialist roles results in more women being successfully chatted-up. His theories have been applied and perfected by rugby teams who divide the tasks up between themselves into manageable chunks so that they can frighten and appal as many women as possible in the pub after a match. In a typical team, two or three will be chosen to pour beer over themselves, another will vomit on his shirt, while three more demonstrate how to drink lager through their noses. A further two members will stand on a table and drop their trousers in order that everyone present can help them search for their lost appendages, while a couple more will sing songs that have no tunes, and no lyrics other than swearing. In this way, all the necessary component parts of chatting-up women (rugby player style) can be carried out

Teamwork

quickly and efficiently, ensuring that not a single man amongst them has the remotest chance of scoring.

If there are only two of you, teamwork can still be a useful way of getting things started. Saying, *my friend fancies you* is pretty corny, but it gets straight to the point without putting potential sparring partners in the ring together before they know they want to fight.

More subtle enquiries can yield useful information. A friend can chat to a friend of the girl you are interested in, to find out basic information such as whether she is single, how old she is, does she do it? You will then be able to begin your chat-up armed with a useful range of conversation topics:

You: So, I understand you're single, you're nineteen, and you do it. Single, eh? What's it like being single?

Her: You should know.

You: Yeh. And you're nineteen. Wow. What's it like being nineteen?

Her: You may never get the chance to find out.

You: Cheers. And you, er, you do it. What's it like?

Her: I refer you to the answer I gave some moments ago.

Teamwork and chatting-up were made for each other. With teamwork, the confidence level is doubled, the embarrassment level is halved, and the success rate is quartered.

 # **Targeting**

With the number of women in the world exceeding the number of men by many millions, we are, apparently, spoilt for choice. On closer inspection, however, it becomes clear that more than ninety per cent of these *surplus* women are over eighty years of age and live in a small mountain village in China. The remaining *surplus* consists of lesbians and nuns. But despite this, situations do arise in which men have the luxury of choice, and when this happens they must carefully *target* their prospective partners in crime.

When there is more than one female available for a potential chat-up, (if, for example, you have successfully gatecrashed a dormitory party in a girls' boarding school), spend a few minutes deciding which one will offer the best chances. The initial short-list will be dictated by your personal taste: her age, fashion style, number of teeth, etc. You must then decide who you have a realistic chance with. If this cuts the list to zero, start again and be a little more optimistic.

If you are inexperienced and are on a chatting-up mission for the first time, remember you don't learn to drive in a Rolls Royce. Save it until your experience gives you the confidence to go for that sort of person. You won't get the necessary experience, however, if you spend your time asking for driving lessons in that Rolls Royce.

When you have chosen who you want to talk to, and have made the first approach, work on her unless or until the signs turn negative, then target someone else. Don't keep flogging a dead horse. If she decides she doesn't want to continue chatting you up, it may be because the lights have come back on and she realises that she finds you physically repulsive,

or it may be that she is meeting her violently jealous boyfriend in a few minutes and must reluctantly let you go. Forget her. Work on the next one, and keep your options open.

Don't be tempted to move in boldly on the girl leaning against the wall looking lonely. She loves watching her boyfriend win fights, and will flirt remorselessly with you until her boyfriend comes out of the toilet, grunts 'Hello', grabs your hand with his piss-stained paw and crushes you like a lemon.

Types to go for/avoid

When choosing a prospective lover, look for firm buttocks, strong shoulders and thick wool, not too tangled. Avoid sheep with horns or ones sprayed with the words *unfit for human conception*.

It's usually possible to filter out those who are *on for a bit* from those whose only sexual knowledge has come from watching *Carry On* films. Look at their clothes, their hairstyles and their general demeanours. Do they want you or what? Are they wearing wedding rings or fertility charms? Could your own charms make her fertile? Don't waste time and effort on raving feminists: they're omnipresent, but harmless — they just get in the way of a man doing his job.

Older women

There is a branch of philosophy which says all that men want out of life is 'Cash, gash, pie 'n' mash,' though not necessarily in that order. If this is true, it is often the older woman who is able to supply it. Sexual experience, confidence and financial security make older women such attractive propositions that younger men can often be seen queuing to do any kind of voluntary work at old people's rest homes.

Some women get sexier as they mature, others do not stand the test of time so well. It is rare to find someone who is perfectly preserved, except for some ancient Egyptians. An older woman with children makes life interesting, particularly if she turns out to have an irresistible daughter of your own age, or perhaps older. This kind of scenario is enough to put years on you. Her years.

Married women

Schoolboy: Sir, my girlfriend's three months pregnant. Is it safe to have sex with her?

Teacher: Only if her husband doesn't find out.

Falling for a married woman is very easy, but coping with the relationship is complicated. If a married woman sees you as her ticket to a more exciting life, tread very carefully. If you don't tread carefully, then at least take off your shoes before you enter the house.

Young girls

Within legal limitations, younger women are uniquely challenging. On the one hand they are inexperienced, inhibited, unworldly and unqualified, but on the other . . . well, it's just their bodies, really. A young body is great, provided you don't want to get a decent conversation out of it. Not that most men would be bothered by that, anyway.

Pretty girls

Going out with a pretty girl is great for the ego, and is bound to make your friends jealous. Until she sleeps with them, too. Chatting-up a pretty girl is always harder psychologically — it's like climbing a bigger mountain than usual. But don't be afraid of trying to conquer her mountain range, you may find that she gets fewer men approaching her than other women simply because most men don't aim that high.

If you decide to go for a pretty girl, just be aware that she will be used to being spoilt by rich boyfriends. If your four poster bed is just a single mattress with four Abba posters on the wall, don't bother. If you pester famous people you meet in the street, rather than *them* begging for an autograph from *you*, don't bother. If you would have to consult with your bank manager before offering to take your lady to Paris for lunch, don't bother. Impetuous, wealthy, high flyers best know how to treat pretty girls.

Ugly girls

Go on, give them a go. No one looks at the mantelpiece when they're stoking the fire, after all.

Teacher/student affairs

If you're slipping behind in your studies, this can be a great way to push up your marks. Those intimate tutorials, the hours spent close to each other talking bollocks, the sense of struggling together to bring you up to scratch intellectually — all this can pull a student and a teacher passionately together.

The trouble is that such relationships are often doomed to secrecy and a feeling of sordidness (nothing wrong with that, of course). Your exam results will improve temporarily, but once your tutor moves on to the next young stud you'll be back to spanking the monkey until it can't take any more abuse.

Sex

A tricky subject, particularly for men - who have to do all the work. Making love (as women like to call it) or shagging requires physical dexterity, subtlety, suppleness and tact. In theory men should try to stimulate more than one erogenous zone (their own zones don't count) at a time whilst 'making love'. This is not easy when you've already got one hand on the television remote control and you can't remember which hand's supposed to be looking for a button.

To make love to a woman's satisfaction, either hire a professional to take your place (there's an address at the beginning of this book) or switch off the television for the necessary duration. You'll probably miss only one or two adverts anyway, so it's usually worth the effort.

Making love is all about being considerate to the woman. Ask her where her 'pleasure spot' is. If she says 'Blackpool' you'll be able to forget about making love and try for a shag instead. But even when just shagging, try not to channel hop too much: women can get awfully sensitive about such things.

It can be fun to tease a woman during sex, perhaps by pretending you're not going to pay her. If you are inexperienced in these matters, the best approach when you get into bed is to be entirely honest. No woman who cares remotely for you will be patronising or unkind if you don't know which hole to aim for or can't put a condom on without reading the instructions on the packet (make sure you pick up the right packet — she won't appreciate you trying to make a soup at a time like this) or if you give her an ice-cream when she asks for a 69.

Don't be too adventurous on your first date. She may not be inclined to be tossed around the bedroom as part of your sexual routine. It is also unwise to unleash the full potential of your sexual repertoire all at once, otherwise she may demand this all the time (what a drag).

There will always be girls who remain under the impression that virginity is a desirable state — until they finally lose it. For men, the opposite applies. Virginity is a heavy burden for a man to carry, like having a heavy sign hanging from your neck that reads 'I am a virgin'. That is until you lose it, when you wonder what all the fuss was about.

Love

People say that 'money can't buy love'. Not for them, it can't, simply because they can't afford it. Love nevertheless flourishes without financial assistance among the poor. Love overpowers hearts, upsets stomachs, and causes diarrhoea in even the hardiest constitutions. Starting with *love at first sight*, love develops into strange, absent-minded behaviour, before finally melting into a pot of indifference soup.

So what is love at first sight? How does it occur? The answer is simply that it doesn't exist. It's actually *lust* at first sight, a strong, overwhelming emotion that is hard to distinguish from love. Lust is short-lived, easy-in, easy-out. *Love* tends to last a little longer. *True love* can last all day.

How to tell if you have genuinely fallen in love:

Toilet roll test

The most objective test is the *toilet roll test*. Make a note of your rate of toilet roll consumption, and if it increases suddenly during a seven day period then you're in love (either with a woman or with your toilet).

Size of your tip test

The next best test is the *size of your tip test*. The size of your tip will increase when you fall in love, so look carefully and see if this is the case. The best place to perform the *size of your tip test* is in a restaurant with your lady friend. If you tip the waiter more generously than usual, you're in love.

Baby test

The *baby test* can be performed by looking at someone else's baby. If you smile at it, you're in love. If you growl until it cries, you're not in love. And probably never will be.

How to write a love letter

Messages of love are more often communicated by fax, e-mail or by sheets hanging from motorway bridges than by letters these days. The only letters that most of us write are to bank managers and these are rarely of a romantic nature (unless you have a fetish for numbers).

If you fill your love letter with romantic slobbering it will be too soggy to post. Keep it dry and crispy so that it retains its shape during its long, arduous journey to the doormat of your loved one.

But how do you *write* a love letter? Basically, you pick up a pen, and drag the moist end of it over a blank sheet of paper in such a way that inky shapes remain on the paper. These are *words*. Make sure you use the words *your*, *love*, *I*, and *jugs* in any letter. These are the raw materials of love letter

writing, and can be used in different orders to tell her how you feel:

Your jugs I love

I love your jugs

Jugs love I your.

If you can draw a picture of the object of your desires, then so much the better. If not, just cut out a photo of a similar pair. She'll be flattered.

For a romantic end to the letter, sellotape a pubic hair to the bottom of the page with the message, *there's plenty more where that came from, luv*. Wipe the letter across your armpit to give it a 'sexy' aroma, pop it in the post, sit back and wait for the response. The police will probably be around in no time.

How to write a love poem

Writing a good love poem is no guarantee of success with women. Shakespeare wrote some of the best gooey rubbish that's ever been written, but his track record with the chicks is certainly nothing to write about. If you need to write a poem for her, the best approach is to use lots of classical imagery. Drop in names of Greek and Roman classical gods, and compare the girl's attributes to the levels of perfection personified by such gods. Don't be tempted to modernise it and compare her to your favourite footballer or supermodel — she won't be impressed.

An alternative approach is to take an existing love poem and adapt it to your needs. If she's the sort of woman who thinks Marvell wrote superhero comics, you could very likely get away with this.

If you have to write an original poem, use her name in the poem, several times if possible, to make her feel that you wrote it just for her. Never use a photocopied poem in which a gap, which has been left for the woman's name, has been filled in with biro.

An ideal poem, Ode to Jane, is printed overleaf:

Ode to Jane

Oh Jane, Jane, Jane,
You drive me insane, Jane,
With your jugs and your newly flushed drain;
Oh how wonderful to be with you again, Jane.

Oh Jane, Jane, Jane,
When my funds began to wane,
I looked for you in vain,
And I was forced to explain
To my bank manager that I needed a loan.

But now I am no longer alone
Because I can hear you moan,
Reverberating through my brain, Jane,
Your voice as sweet as a sugar cane, Jane.
It truly would be a calamity, Jane,
If you were to abandon me again, Jane.
So don't.

How to write a love song

Instead of getting a tattoo featuring your favourite lady's name and an eagle, why not write a song about her? In each art form, tattoo and song, the lady is named, but the latter genre carries less stigma when you change your mind and fall in love with her best friend. When it gets to the point when your arm resembles a page from a telephone directory, you may wish you had chosen to write a song for them all instead. Love songs also enable you to write about the whole of womankind in one go — it's a bit like having 'I love birds' tattooed on your arm, only more respectable.

You don't have to be musical to write a love song. Ten minutes listening to Radio 1 is proof of that. Just buy a keyboard or a guitar, sit in front of the tape recorder and make some sounds. Grunt the magic words, *I love your jugs* several times over, bang a saucepan unnecessarily loudly throughout the song, and simmer for three minutes. Serve with garnish and red wine.

How to act
in front of her parents

Meeting a girl's parents for the first time can be a harrowing experience. Her father will inevitably be an army major with eyebrows that overhang like a pair of woolly ski jumps, who has an air of disgust that makes you feel small enough to fit inside the living ecosystem of his furry nostrils, and whose barking voice sends you cowering behind the curtains. How did someone like that ever produce such a lovely daughter, you wonder? Her beautiful mother will be the answer to that question, and the cause of the next dilemma: you fancy her more than her daughter . . .

You will never be good enough for their daughter, so it's probably not worth trying. Whatever you do for a living, however neatly you dress or how well you speak, in the back of their minds will always be the thought that you are molesting their precious little girl. You are sullying their clean household, breaking up the family and destroying their daughter's innocence. How can you possibly relax in front of them when you know this is what they are thinking?

Most girlfriend's parents will delve into your background when you first meet. Some will even have an *eligibility questionnaire* prepared for you to complete, the results of which will be pinned up on a wall with hundreds of others on their daughter's twenty-first birthday.

When staying at a girlfriend's house while her parents are there, the main problem is the sleeping arrangement. You may have spent ninety-nine out of a hundred nights at college sharing a single bed with her, but at her house you will not

be allowed within a mile of her double bed. There is nothing you can do about this other than sneak into her room at night provided the floorboards and bedsprings are quiet enough. However, show some respect to her parents wishes by making sure you don't get caught.

When things turn sour . . .

What can you do if the girl of your dreams turns out after a few dates to be mildly less interesting than Radio 3 on a quiet night? Do you take out a full page advertisement in her favourite newspaper telling her you think she's boring and you never want to see her again? Do you daub her with red paint and drag her through the streets so that everyone knows she is impure? Or do you take her to a restaurant, buy her an expensive meal, explain carefully why you think the relationship isn't working, and then carry out the first two options?

Ending a relationship without pain is like getting served in a pub on a Saturday night. Impossible. All you can do is to let her down as gently as you can, and hope she doesn't revengefully blab your personal secrets to all of her friends.

How To Chat-up Women

A good way to do this is to try a *trial separation*. You suggest a limited time to be apart from each other, say forty years, after which you have the option to get back together and assess the situation. This method enables you to get rid of her without actually letting her down completely.

Rejection by letter or fax is a useful means of setting out clearly and logically your reasons for splitting up. It doesn't give her the chance to interrupt and put you off, but it's pretty impersonal, particularly if you head the letter *Dear Sir/Madam*.

If you sense your relationship is heading towards a dead-end, ie. marriage, it's best to nip it in the bud as soon as possible before it's too late.

The 21 best chat-up lines in the world . . .

I can read you like a book. I bet you're great between the covers.

What winks and is great in bed?

I don't know.

(Wink)

Do you want to come back to my place for a pizza and a shag? No? Why, don't you like pizza?

It's getting late. Why don't we have a shag?

No thanks, I'm too tired.

Well would you mind lying down while I have one?

When I was a prisoner of war
they tortured me on the rack,
and it wasn't just my legs
they stretched . . .

The best thing about you would have to be . . . my arms.

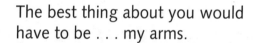

(Call her over using your finger)
I made you come using just one finger. Imagine what I could do with my whole hand!

Nice legs. When do they open?

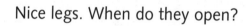

I'm like quick-drying cement: after I've been laid it doesn't take me long to get hard.

You'd probably regret it in the morning if we slept together, I suppose. So how about we sleep together in the afternoon?

Hello, you don't know me, but I've just come back from the future in which you and me have the most passionate love affair. And it started tonight, actually.

Hi, I'm from Wonderbra. We're conducting free spot checks to make sure our customers are wearing the correct size bras. Just breathe out slowly once my hands are in place . . .

Hi, I'm a policeman, but that's not a truncheon . . .

There's something on your face, I think it's beauty. Let me try and get it off . . . oh, it's not coming off.

I'm a postman, so you can rely on me to deliver a large package.

I bet you a drink that you won't kiss me.

Hello, I'm your cake. Would you like to have it or eat it?

Mind if I plug my lap-top into your modem socket?

If I told you I was well endowed in the undercarriage department, would you shag me?

No.

Good, because I'm actually very small.

You make me feel like a squirrel. Mind
if I pile my nuts up against you.

What are you doing for the
next millennium?

Epilogue

To end this book I would like to summarise a few important points. Being single is the not the end of the world, but it's dangerously close to Outer Mongolia. Eight out of ten philosophers agree that the most important thing in life is to be happy. Eight out of ten mechanics agree that the second most important thing is to service your car regularly. In third place, it is vital to service your relationship every 12,000 miles. Remember that being in a relationship will not automatically bring happiness, but if regularly maintained it should give you years of trouble-free rides.

Relationships and playing the game of forming relationships can be fun. Whether you are meeting girls through dating agencies, mutual friends or as strangers in a pub, have fun. And if she won't let you have fun, she's probably just practising for when you get married.

Here are some *don'ts* to send you on your merry way:

1. Don't be square but don't be so fashionable that your clothes appear to be inside out and your hair looks like a toilet brush.

2. Don't force your attentions on her but don't simply force them on yourself each night, either.

3. Don't excessively flatter her but don't throw a bucket of paint over her.

4. Don't have unpleasant body odour but don't wear so much after-shave that you smell like a perfume factory.

5. Don't talk about yourself all evening but don't be so moody and silent that she guesses you've got something to hide.

6. Don't be flashy but don't be dull.

7. Don't dismiss what she talks about as trivial but don't pander obsequiously to her every word.

8. Don't mention how well you get on with the nurses at the local VD clinic, but don't bother showing her the results of a recent medical to prove you're up to the job.

9. Don't panic!

10. **Don't think for a moment that anything in this book will actually improve your chances!**

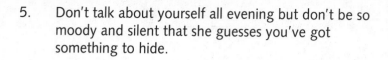

Epilogue

Other Humour Books from Summersdale

Chat-up Lines and Put Downs
Stewart Ferris £3.99

More Chat-up Lines and Put Downs
Stewart Ferris £3.99

How To Chat-up Men (Pocket edition)
Kitty Malone £3.99

Enormous Boobs
The Greatest Mistakes In The History of the World
Stewart Ferris £4.99

101 Uses for a Losing Lottery Ticket
Shovel/Nadler £3.99

Men!
Can't Live with them, Can't live *with* them
Tania Golightly £3.99

Girl Power
Kitty Malone £3.99

The Kama Sutra For One
O'Nan and P. Palm
£3.99

101 Reasons Not To Do Anything
A Collection of Cynical and Defeatist Quotations
£3.99

A Little Bathroom Book £3.99

Available from all good bookshops.